The way of Lament

DR TERRY BOYLE

INSIGHT FOR LIVING
UNITED KINGDOM

The Way of Lament
by Dr Terry Boyle

Dr Terry Boyle serves as Pastor for Insight for Living UK. His ministry involves teaching a weekend radio programme, hosting the weekday *Insight for Living* broadcast, helping with issues that come in from listeners, and providing a personal and local approach to the international Bible-teaching ministry of Charles R. Swindoll.

Pastor Terry was born in Windsor, England. He moved to the United States in 1981. Although he began his professional life as a biochemist, Terry holds a Th.M. in Pastoral Ministry and a Ph.D. in Biblical Studies from Dallas Theological Seminary. He served as senior pastor of Skillman Bible Church in Dallas, Texas until he and his family moved back to the United Kingdom in 2007.

Copyright © 2012 by Terry Boyle
First printed in 2012. This edition printed in 2013.

Published by Insight for Living UK, PO Box 553, Dorking, RH4 9EU

Editor in Chief: Terry Boyle, Pastor, Insight for Living UK
Executive Director: Scott Bean, Insight for Living UK
Editors: Jonathan Shulver and Philip Sweeting
Cover Designer and Production Artist: Mike Watermeyer, Communications Specialist, Insight for Living UK
Design Editor: Karen Sawrey, Designer, www.karensawrey.com
Cover Photo: iStockphoto

ISBN: 978-0-9571571-0-1

Printed in the United Kingdom

In the Lord I take refuge;

. . .

The Lord is in his holy temple;

the Lord's throne is in heaven;

his eyes see, his eyelids test the children of man.

The Lord tests the righteous,

but his soul hates the wicked and the one who loves violence.

Psalm 11 v 11 (ESV)

Contents

Introduction

The Bible has many examples of desperate prayers cried out to God from the pit of anguish. These are most easily found in the Book of Psalms, where the mood of about half of the book presents itself to us from the viewpoint of someone in distress. Just think: the Bible's own book of praise devotes half of its attention to expressing the fears and pains of life on earth. This is a helpful clue to us all. If these "songs of hard times" are any indication, then God is neither surprised nor offended when we come to Him with our troubles. Just knowing this gives us courage and hope when we find ourselves on the receiving end of life's harsh realities. Courage to bring our pain to Him as the psalmists have done, and hope in the assurance that, through Christ, God the Father is fully acquainted with our griefs and sorrows. Christ knew what it was to be hungry, homeless, tempted, betrayed and even mortally wounded. So God really knows what it feels like to live life on this earth as a human being.

Trouble is Trouble, No Matter How You Look at It

Sometimes trouble comes seemingly out of nowhere – a bad report from the doctor, a serious accident or some unexpected turn of events that leaves us feeling shocked, panicky and powerless. Any and all of us can list off times when things just didn't seem fair; times when it felt as though God has fallen asleep on the job. If that way of thinking seems a little irreverent to you, consider these lines from Psalm 44, verses 23-24:

Awake! Why are you sleeping, O Lord?
Rouse yourself! Do not reject us forever!

Why do you hide your face?
Why do you forget our affliction and oppression?

Like most pastors, I can clearly recall moments when I have prayed with parents over the death of their child and also when I have comforted young children in the loss of a parent. My own daughter's life once hung in the balance after a car accident. Dreadful diseases, harsh betrayals and terrible disasters can strike out of a blue sky and there is no apparent rhyme or reason to them. The pain penetrates us to the marrow; confusion and doubt overwhelm our thoughts. At such times, those words from Psalm 44 are often hovering in the back of my mind.

There are other times – let's be honest – when trouble comes upon us because we have behaved badly and we have not used godly wisdom. These are the times when the theme tune to our lives is "I Did It My Way." You don't have to read far in the Book of Proverbs before you realise that "There is a way that seems right to a man, but its end is the way to death." (Proverbs 14:12 and 16:25). This self-inflicted trouble comes in many shapes and guises. Bad health and a shortened life brought upon by substance abuse; a season in jail for improper financial dealings; the unravelling of a family when secret affairs are brought to light. But these are just the consequences, the public collateral damage of our personal, inward rebellion. Often these consequences cannot be reversed but the wrong thinking that put them into motion can be. It's called repentance.

Like the Prodigal Son, when we finally come to our senses and see things clearly, we desperately want to be restored to our Father's care, but can't think of a way back. The soul pain is just as real even when it's our own fault. Guilt, regret and shame weigh us down and cause a kind of spiritual paralysis. We feel unclean, unworthy, and unacceptable. Going to church (if we even go) is a dark ordeal rather than a celebration, and the last thing we want to see is an open Bible! God's hand feels heavy upon us, and we know something must give – but how can we approach our holy and righteous Father when we've made such a mess of things?

The appropriate, biblical approach to God in times of pain – either pain of our own making or pain from the chaos of a fallen world – is the Way of Lament.

The General Shape of Lament

We are trained from a very early age to recognise certain kinds of literature, and we learn to expect certain things from each kind. A piece of writing that begins "Once upon a time…" is quickly categorised as a children's story, while the words "Dear Sir or Madam…" suggest a rather formal letter. We have a good idea of what "shape" the following sentences will take. We don't expect the letter from the bank to be signed off with "…and they all lived happily ever after" any more than we expect the bed-time tale to close with "Yours Faithfully."

These same ideas about what to expect from particular kinds of literature also hold true when we come to the Bible. Within the sixty-six books we discover categories such as historical narratives, royal archives, poems, accounts of visions and dreams, proverbs, and even morality plays (such as some of the extended scenes in Proverbs 1-9). All these different kinds of writing need to be understood on their own terms.

Within the category of poetry we find the Psalms, and one kind of poetry we frequently see there is best described as Lament. Although there is a great deal of variety in how grief is expressed in the Psalms, there are some underlying patterns –

features that many psalms of Lament seem to share. Like children's stories and letters from the bank, Lament has a shape of its own, so to speak.[1] Some of the consistent features we can expect to find are these:

- A brief, desperate cry to God: there's no time to waste when you're in pain.

- A complaint: something has gone wrong, and life hurts.

- A confession: this can either be a cry of innocence: "This isn't my fault!" or a cry of guilt: "I brought this on myself!"

- An appeal for action: the action item is often dependent on whether the petition is from innocence: "deal sternly with my enemies, O God!" or from guilt: "be merciful to me O Lord!"

- An expression of praise: confidence in God's character and faithfulness.

It has been my experience, in both teaching the Psalms in the classroom and in providing pastoral care, that this general shape can be a very helpful frame upon which to hang our own grief and pain. Using the Psalms of Lament as our guide, we can begin to give a voice to our disappointments and losses, our setbacks and regrets. We can shape our prayers in such a way that we neither take on false guilt, nor whitewash over our own mistakes. Lament is biblical but it is also raw and honest. You won't find much beating around the bush in the psalms we will use for guidance. We look to them to give us the courage to speak out what we really feel when life hurts.

---

1. Ground-breaking technical work in this field was developed by Claus Westermann: (Westermann 1980).

Lament When It's Not My Fault

We all know the dismay of living in a fallen world. Things happen out of the blue for which we can find no reason, and for which we are not to blame. The temptation is sometimes to blame ourselves anyway. A child is lost to a drunk driver, and we fret that we should have taken a different way home; a global financial meltdown causes life-savings to evaporate overnight, and we stress ourselves out rehashing decisions that were made years ago, and seemed well-advised and wise at the time. Rape, cancer, persecution and violence – any number of dreadful things can steal our security and shake our world, even challenge our faith. How do we speak to God when He seems far off, when life hurts and it's not our fault? Let's look at two psalms; one from David – Psalm 11, and another whose author is not revealed to us, we will know him as the *afflicted one* – Psalm 102.

Psalm 11: When the Wicked Seem to Have the Upper Hand

It's impossible to know with certainty what prompted David to write this short, pithy prayer. But there are some clues given to us in the psalm that can give us an idea of his situation. The first thing we notice is that he is turning down advice. Someone has suggested that he should run away from his trouble. Here is what David has been told:

> *"Flee like a bird to your mountain,*
> *for behold, the wicked bend the bow;*
> *they have fitted their arrow to the string*
> *to shoot in the dark at the upright in heart;*
> *if the foundations are destroyed,*
> *what can the righteous do?"*

David's advisors raise serious concerns. Their fear is that he will come to harm, and they paint a picture of archers hiding in the shadows on the brink of an assassination attempt. In today's world we would say things like "there's trouble in every dark alley, and the risk of violence lurks around every corner." If the righteous *(the upright in heart)* can be threatened in this way, what hope is there for society? That's what they mean by the phrase "if the foundations are destroyed." The idea is that there is no power of law or sense of justice in the land. The bedrock of civilisation is that decent people, good people, kings or paupers, should be safe in their homes and on their streets. If that isn't the case, then the fainthearted are tempted to just give up and run. That's the advice they gave to David at least.

The problems described by David's advisors actually sound quite modern and familiar. Today the news reports chant a steady litany of violence and injustice worked against the innocent. We read about muggings, stabbings and burglaries, and we fret about whether it's safe even to walk down to the chip shop. We learn of wickedness at the top and the bottom of our culture. There is a kind of fear that sets in whose main effect is to paralyse us, to steal our confidence and to suppress our joy. We've all felt it. This short psalm expresses our emotions so clearly. We are very familiar with the daily oppression of life in a society where decent, honest people come to harm through no fault of their own.

This is our complaint to God: we are reluctant to leave our homes, it feels to us like the wicked and the lawless rule the streets, there is an overwhelming sense that decency and honesty are on the losing side. Deep inside, we want to run away. They are hard words to say, but they are important to give voice to because they are true. Lament is all about getting our complaint out in the open, to give it air. We have an expectation of how society is supposed to work, and ours is broken on many levels. Not spoken – but implied in our thinking – is the subversive notion that God has let us down. What do we do with that?

David is clear and firm in his response to the advice of his counsellors. How can they possibly think that running and hiding is the best way forward? Notice that in the lines following their complaint he doesn't deny their analysis, he only objects to their solution. Their advice comes from a too-small view of God. He will not run away or back down because even if it is as bad as they say, his security is in God, not in society:

In the Lord I take refuge;

. . .

The Lord is in his holy temple;
the Lord's throne is in heaven;
his eyes see, his eyelids test the children of man.
The Lord tests the righteous,
but his soul hates the wicked and the one who loves violence.

David reminds his unnamed friends that God is not "out of the loop." He has not been startled from His throne by the notion that there are wicked men at work, nor is there a sign on the door of heaven that reads "on holiday, back in two weeks." God's sovereignty is neither interrupted nor threatened! What a tough lesson that is to learn when the world seems to be in such a mess. David takes the big view of a big God, and even while human society rattles off its gimbals, he knows that nothing will shake the Lord. In fact, while we go about our daily lives – whether in God's graces or turning our hands to evil – God isn't missing a trick. He tests mankind as a goldsmith would assay a box of rare coins. Is it gold . . . or is it scrap? Both the righteous and the wicked are tested, and the results of God's evaluations are never wrong. The works of the cruel, the faithless, the disgraceful and the disgusting will not be allowed to slip by unnoticed.

Run away and hide? What good would that accomplish? If all the good folks opt out, who then will stand for righteousness? That seems to be David's mind-set. It's a courageous attitude. Needless to say, it comes across as foolhardy to those with a too-small view of God, but it's a stand we can all take in some way. Edmund Burke is given credit for the much-used expression "All that is necessary for the triumph of evil is that good men do nothing." But what are good men and women to do? David calls on God to act. He prays quite deliberately for God to make the lives of the wicked miserable:

Let him rain coals on the wicked;
fire and sulphur and a scorching wind shall be the portion of their cup.

David's prayer strikes our modern sensibilities as a bit mean-spirited. But is it really? On a radio programme I heard recently, the issue of thugs and petty burglars was being discussed. One of the correspondents remarked in passing that she hoped they (the offenders) could sleep at night. I knew what she intended to mean but I was jolted to the realisation that that is exactly the last thing I want for them. I want them to be miserable, not comfortable. I want them to suffer torment in the conscience of their soul; I want the thugs and thieves and the muggers and the rapists to go long nights without rest or peace or enjoyment. It's not mean, and it's not uncharitable, it's honest. It simply doesn't make sense to want the wicked to enjoy an easy life. The psalms are full of the notion that decent people long for the rascals to get what's coming to them.

In the long run, of course, I want God to get their attention and bring them to repentance. For many people a season of hardship is what it takes to open the door to remorse and redemption. It is society itself that has been given the responsibility of being God's agent in this. Governments are appointed, administrations are established whose task is to work justice, and their work is sanctioned by God. The Apostle Paul is clear in Romans 13 that human government "does not carry the sword in vain" but is to be respected and even feared by those who break the law. There is no shame in praying for the wicked to find justice and to find it swiftly. Mercy is a commendable virtue, but true mercy is not the same as pretending there has been no offence; that's denial, a completely dishonest approach to justice. For mercy even to be considered, there first needs to be an admission of guilt.

Then, taking Ephesians 4:28 as my model, I would want to see the offender work hard to restore what they have taken, to rebuild what they have destroyed and to become of some use to the society they have betrayed and tried to undermine. Take careful note that this season of chastening, even though we can pray earnestly for it to come about, is left up to God in terms of the ways and means. By praying this, we place the burden in His lap, there is no room for private human vengeance here.

The closing lines of Psalm 11 bring us back to the firm ground of God's character and His response towards those who choose good over evil. It's important to remind ourselves that God's favour is the ultimate reward and righteousness is the ultimate motive. It's essential to understand that just as there will be sure justice administered to the wayward, there is peace and blessing awaiting those who seek God out:

> *For the Lord is righteous;*
> *he loves righteous deeds;*
> *the upright shall behold his face.*

This promise is even extended to the ones who have bent the bow, fitted the arrow, and sought to kill us – either in thought, word or deed. We were all there once. According to 1 Corinthians 6:10-11, we were all strangers to God and rebels against His ways:

> *...nor thieves, nor the greedy, nor drunkards, nor revilers, nor swindlers*

will inherit the kingdom of God. And such were some of you.
But you were washed, you were sanctified, you were justified
in the name of the Lord Jesus Christ and by the Spirit of our God.

How, Then, Should We Pray?

The privilege of God's love, and the delight of being close to Him, these are treasures indeed. They are treasures that are found only through Christ. There is no real righteousness outside of Him. How then should we pray, when it appears that the wicked have the upper hand, when we are afraid that our society has become toxic? If we follow David's lead:

- ***We must be resolved to stand firm,*** to remind ourselves that our own security only lies in the safekeeping of God's character. Finding our safety there, we will not feel the need to run away in the face of tough times – our steadfastness is tied directly to how we view God.

- ***We need to be honest about what we ask the Lord to do.*** Emotional honesty comes as such a breath of fresh air in our prayer life. We don't want the wicked to prosper but they often do for a while. We can genuinely, and with clear intention, ask God to keep them miserable and tormented until they come to their senses and turn to Him in remorse and repentance. When we have given that burden to God, perhaps we can then honestly let go of our hunger for personal vengeance. And when we are free of the need for vengeance, we can even rejoice when the wicked are redeemed.

- ***We can sincerely thank God.*** Even though we once were as far from Him as the wicked are now, God has called us to His side as friends, and that is the safest place to be no matter what goes on around us.

Psalm 102: When Good People Are Suffering

Some of the psalms carry a superscription; it's a little note before the actual text begins that sets the scene. The superscription for Psalm 102 says this:

> *A prayer of one afflicted, when he is faint*
> *and pours out his complaint before the Lord.*

It's worth noting at the outset that there is nothing in this psalm to suggest that the "one afflicted" has done anything to deserve the suffering they are going through. He or she is like so many of our friends, family and church members who are struck with illness or tragedy for no apparent reason. Life in this fallen world is full of collateral damage, the indiscriminate shrapnel of sin that cuts into us all.

We don't know who this was – *the afflicted one* – but we know people like him well enough. The young mum who went into the hospital for a minor procedure and picked up a resistant infection; the teenager hit by a car on the way home from football practice; the hardworking husband whose job has just been outsourced; the one whose life is grinding down to a brutal stop with MS or Motor Neurone Disease; he is the blameless victim. And like so many victims, his first complaint is that he feels God-forsaken. He doesn't believe that the Lord is paying attention to his troubles:

> *Hear my prayer, O Lord; let my cry come to you!*
> *Do not hide your face from me in the day of my distress!*
> *Incline your ear to me; answer me speedily in the day when I call!*

Where is God when I need Him most? Why does He seem to stand so far off? What is God up to in all of this? Why doesn't He do something? Quietly, and often with a sense of muted embarrassment, these questions tumble in the back of our minds. We are afraid to give voice to our frustration in case it is going to be taken as a failure of faith. But once again, we will find that emotional honesty is a crucial part of lament.

Let's look first at the catalogue of afflictions woven through the fabric of this prayer. The victim relates his suffering using a series of poetic images. He feels burned up like smoke and fire (v3); he is too miserable to eat and he sees the consequences, it's as though his bones are sticking to his skin (v4-5); he can't sleep, he says he is like a nocturnal bird in the wilderness (v6), but more than that – keeping with his image of birds – he is exposed and vulnerable like a sparrow on a rooftop, a favourite target for pot-shots. These pot-shots aren't stones though. They are the taunts and jeers of the people who hate him (v8). How they love to see his misery! In fact he makes a prime example of how they want their other targets to end up. They use his name like a bad-luck charm against the other people they hate – "you know such-and-such? I hope you end up just like him!" To sum it all up, he feels his life ebbing away, there is nothing left to live for, nothing left to live on. But the most hurtful symptom of them all? – it feels as if God has just thrown him away in a fit of spite (v10).

Fevers, malnourishment, insomnia and fearful vulnerability – all of these might be tolerable for a time. But how many of us can tolerate that haunting suspicion that God is actually behind our misery? How many of us are even willing to confess that we suspect it? The notion is that God not only allows suffering but even brings it down on His people, ruining their health, stealing their peace of mind and wrecking their reputation. If it's God Himself we are up against in times of trouble, well what chance do we have? It's the thinking process of a mind in absolute despair, completely demoralised by circumstances, overwhelmed by pain. It's the voice of depression. At that moment, in such extreme distress, God seems to be mean and vindictive. We picture Him as a capricious and fickle tyrant toying with His creatures. He is more like the petty gods of Greek mythology than the One True God of creation.

It isn't true of course, but it *feels* true at the time, and it has to be given voice, even shouted out; it has to be expressed. Emotional honesty demands it.

You might speak to people who have suffered a serious tragedy or been struck down with some debilitating illness and you will often hear them say that they went through a period where they were furious at God, blaming Him for their pain and disappointment. Joni Eareckson[2], paralysed by a simple diving accident at seventeen years of age, expressed it this way: "I was despondent, but I was also angry because of my helplessness. How I wished for strength and control enough in my fingers to do something, anything, *to end my life*."[3]

C. S. Lewis carefully evaluated his pain and confusion in the months following the all-too-soon death of Joy Gresham, his wife of just four years: "…But go to Him [God] when your need is desperate, when all other help is in vain, and what do you find? A door slammed in your face, and a sound of bolting and double bolting on the inside. After that silence. You may as well turn away."[4]

Is it wrong? Is it a sin to shake a fist at God – to raise questions about His methods and motives? Think of some of the people in the Bible who did. Job springs immediately to mind. Consider his words from the beginning of chapter ten:

I loathe my life;
I will give free utterance to my complaint;
I will speak in the bitterness of my soul.
I will say to God, Do not condemn me;

---

2. You may know her as Joni Eareckson Tada, as she has been known since marrying Ken Tada in 1982, six years after the events described.

3. (Eareckson, Joni 1976)

4. (Lewis 1961)

let me know why you contend against me.
Does it seem good to you to oppress,
to despise the work of your hands
and favour the designs of the wicked?

Job was convinced that God had authored his suffering and he was compelled to demand a fair hearing in the universal court of appeal. Described as "blameless and upright, one who feared God and turned away from evil," Job knew that if God was really behind his troubles, then He had some serious explaining to do. The answer for Job, as it is for all of us, was to re-frame his perspective. And that's where *the afflicted one* takes us in this psalm. Perspective changes everything.

Everyone who travels to Paris for the first time has that one picture that must be taken. It's a photographic cliché, but all holiday albums must have at least one. It's the one with you holding the Eiffel Tower in the palm of your hand, or resting your finger on the point at the top, or just casually leaning against it, or wearing it like a hat. We do the same thing in Pisa, or at Stonehenge or Westminster. Perspective is fun to play with, but when it comes to soul pain, perspective is anything but frivolous. The only way forward is to take a step back; to see the bigger picture.

Now returning to our psalm, look at how *the afflicted one* takes a long step back. In verses 1-11 he is focused only on himself. Count how many times he uses "I," "me," and "my." He is engrossed with a shaving-mirror inspection of his own condition. Then abruptly in verses 12-22, we notice a surprising shift of perspective. Now God and His reputation fill the viewfinder. In widescreen language we are reminded that God is sovereign *forever*, throughout *all* generations; *all* the kings of the earth will fear him. Why? Because He is faithful to His promises. He shows loyal affection for His people. He hears their prayers – even the prayers of those deep in the dungeons of despair.

For the faithful Israelite, God's covenant loyalty was all tied up in thoughts of Jerusalem. The beautiful city, the seat of David and his descendants, the settlement of the Tabernacle and the site of the Temple. That is where the focus moves to, because that city is at the emotional heart of the Hebrew nation. In the psalmist's eyes, the freedom, security, and prosperity of Zion were the vital signs – the pulse and blood pressure – of God's faithfulness.

For many Christian believers, Jerusalem is still a place of great emotional importance; but in terms of the New Covenant and the New Testament Church we have a different focus. Referring to the Temple in Jerusalem, Christ pronounced that "there will not be left here one stone upon another that will not be thrown down." (Matthew 24:2) Clearly there was going to be a change of focus for the faithful. Paul refers in Ephesians chapter two to the:

> ... household of God, built on the foundation of the apostles and prophets,
> Christ Jesus himself being the cornerstone,
> in whom the whole structure, being joined together,
> grows into a holy temple in the Lord.
> In him you also are being built together into
> a dwelling place for God by the Spirit.

So in the Church Age, where we find ourselves today, it is the fellowship of Christian believers all around the world that constitutes the place where God, through His Spirit, meets with mankind. In other words, it is the Church that has become the focus of God's working on earth, and the pulse and blood pressure – the vital signs – of God's faithfulness are presently measured there. That is where our emotional capital is to be invested.

As the petitioner steps back for a new perspective there is a glance back at God's reputation for faithfulness in verse 12, and then a long look forward to a time of hope and renewed blessing. The psalmist has complete confidence that generations to come will be able to praise God for the work He is about to do in this present hour of need. Even if things are bad now, he is sure that God is working in history to bring about victory and justice. Out of a very dark and painful "now" God will bring a bright new "next":

> *Let this be recorded for a generation to come,*
> *so that a people yet to be created may praise the Lord:*
> *that he looked down from his holy height;*
> *from heaven the Lord looked at the earth,*
> *to hear the groans of the prisoners,*
> *to set free those who were doomed to die.*

The afflicted one now returns to his complaint in verse 23, but notice that he is not as bitter or bleak (or as self-absorbed) as when he started out in prayer. Stepping back to get a bigger perspective has changed the way he looks at his life. His own plight has woven itself now into the fabric of a much bigger picture. His situation (even though it has not changed) is now intertwined with God's situation:

> *He has broken my strength in midcourse; he has shortened my days.*
> *"O my God," I say, "take me not away in the midst of my days—*
> *you whose years endure throughout all generations!"*
> *Of old you laid the foundation of the earth,*
> *and the heavens are the work of your hands.*
> *They will perish, but you will remain;*
> *they will all wear out like a garment.*
> *You will change them like a robe, and they will pass away,*
> *but you are the same, and your years have no end.*

It is now a sovereign and eternal Lord, not a spiteful and arbitrary petty god who fills the frame. God is worthy of praise because of who He is, not because of how well we think we are doing. We see that *the afflicted one* is still aware that his life is troubled, even shortened. And he still doesn't like it, but he sees his condition in context now. Somehow God's reputation is being put in front of his own. It's true that in the close-up pain of the moment, our personal hardships loom large. But in the grand scheme of things, in the long view, it is God's universe.

How does praying ourselves into the right perspective help? How do we move forward with each day when each day is so difficult? I mentioned the story of Joni Eareckson earlier, and in her second book *A Step Further*, Joni gives an account of meeting a woman named Nadine. She had severe cerebral palsy. Like Joni, she was confined to a difficult life of wheelchairs and constant care. Here is how Joni described the attitude they shared:

> *...And what is most interesting, she not only tolerates God – she loves Him.*
> *The God she has come to know is so worth knowing, so real, that she*
> *gladly and willingly endures her condition if that's what pleases Him.*
>
> *Does Nadine's suffering glorify God? It sure does. Why?*
> *Because God miraculously removes it?*
> *No, her suffering glorifies God because the people who see and know her*
> *are forced to at least consider the fact that Nadine's Lord*
> *must be somebody special to inspire such loyalty.*[5]

Another woman who has encountered a different kind of suffering is Elisabeth Elliot. You may know something of her story. She and her husband Jim were missionaries in a team outreach to certain tribes in Ecuador. All the men in the

---

5. (Eareckson and Estes, A Step Further 1978)

team, including her husband, were killed. Several years later she married again, and lost her second husband to cancer. Her marriage to Jim was severed in three years, and her second husband, Addison, died in the fourth year of their marriage. Elisabeth took a long step back in order to see the bigger picture:

When I speak of the "gift" of widowhood,
I do not mean that God made us widows.
He did not inspire the Auca Indians to throw their lances,
and then see to it that they found their mark.
He does not give people cancer, cause a baby to be born with deformities,
or persuade husbands and wives to divorce.

These are among the evils which result from man's decision to disobey.
In the Garden of Eden he chose death, as God had plainly told him
beforehand. We are still just as free to choose, and the consequences are
just as inexorable – but so is His love.[6]

Elisabeth, with a "quiet heart"[7] and a steady eye, places the blame exactly where it should be. Pain comes from living in a fallen world. To deny it is futile. Both Joni and Elisabeth, each in her own way, learned the lesson of *the afflicted one*. It is clear from Psalm 102 that even in his misery, *the afflicted one* remains loyal to God. He has every confidence that God, the eternal and unchangeable Lord, will prevail. In his lifetime? Perhaps not, but that is not the issue for him as he closes his prayer. As long as the faithful persevere, God's reputation will pass from generation to generation. The faithful will be vindicated, if not in this brief season on earth, then certainly in all eternity:

The children of your servants shall dwell secure;

---

6. (Elliot, Loneliness 1988)

7. The phrase is borrowed from another of Elisabeth's books: (Elliot, Keep A Quiet Heart 1995)

their offspring shall be established before you.

In other words, if we can keep our perspective when tragedy strikes, our children and our children's children will know something of God's unchanging faithfulness. The way we respond to times – even lifetimes – of suffering speaks volumes to those around us concerning the God we love and serve. Christians are not given promises of health and wealth on this earth. Don't let anyone convince you otherwise. We should not covet these things, nor insist that God has cheated us when we do not get them. He has promised to sustain us through our trials, not rescue us out of the midst of them. A quiet heart and a steady eye fixed on His love will see us through.

How, Then, Should We Pray?

If we take *the afflicted one* as our guide for prayer in seasons of unwarranted pain and tragedy, how should we approach God in our distress? Once again, let me emphasise the importance of emotional honesty. There is a hidden genie in the bottle when we are suffering and it's not our fault. Unless we let out that pent-up idea that God has it in for us – get it off our chest – we can never step back from that "me-centred" viewpoint and take in the big picture. We have to *own* and *confess* our doubts about God's goodness before we can put them in perspective. So here are three stages in a prayer that could take a few moments, a few months, or a few years to work through.

- *Let it out!* By this I don't mean blurting your struggles at the unsuspecting passenger on the bus, or even to the full church on a Sunday morning. This is soul-work and it is essentially between you and God in times of prayer. Your pastor might be the one to go to if you need a sounding-board, or perhaps a trusted friend, or you can journal your pain and disappointment if that way suits you. The important thing to remember is that God is neither surprised nor dismayed by your complaint. He has sanctioned such in the Psalms, and He has heard much worse from the saints who have gone before you. You are not disappointing God by coming to Him with your questions. It is not a failure of faith. Illness, tragedy, pain; these are the currencies of a broken world, and God has not, in His wise timing, brought them to an end yet. The psalmist was careful to dwell on his pain. It was the dominant aspect of his view. For a while it was all he could see.

- *Step back and see the big picture.* Perspective makes all the difference. God works with very long horizons. He is not *obligated* to make our individual lives comfortable or affluent or convenient. He is worthy of praise on the basis of who He is, not on the basis of whether we are happy with the cards we are dealt. He is the unchangeable one, the universal constant. Our suffering is very temporary at worst, but if we overcome with perseverance, our joy will be eternal.

- *Trust God with the big picture outcome.* What do we teach our children from the way we deal with our trials? They watch us more closely than we would like to imagine. Do we keep a "big picture" approach? The psalmist had firm assurance that generations to come would bring glory to God. Not from his self-absorbed preoccupation with his own temporary misery, but from his enduring faith that God was in fact the only unchangeable fixture in the universe. Abiding from age to age and trustworthy even in hard times. I have often spoken to grown men and women who remember back to their childhood and recall with a kind of awe the unwavering, uncomplicated faith of their grandparents, even during wartime and the Great Depression. They say: "That is the kind of faith I want to have, and the kind of faith I want to show my children; the unshakeable faith my grandparents and parents had." Children notice that kind of perspective, and when they hit their own tough seasons, they remember. They remember the God who helped you to persevere, to endure; and they in turn will call upon Him in their time of need.

Lament When It Is My Fault

We have all been there, if we're honest (there's that word again!). A naïve mistake, a foolish lapse in judgment; a period of rebellious stupidity or even a prolonged season of malice or promiscuity. Now guilt, shame and regret have caught up with us. It's time to do some soul-work, but where do we start? How can we make an approach to God when we feel so foolish and foul? Will He even want us back? The songsmith Paul Simon once wrote these words that capture the mood well:

And here I am, Lord
I'm knocking at your place of business
I know I ain't got no business here
But you said if I ever got so low
I was busted,
You could be trusted.[8]

There are several psalms that can shed some light on that very dark place, where we desperately want to knock on God's office door, but are afraid of the reception we'll get when we step in. For now we'll be looking at another psalm from David – Psalm 51. The lines from this prayer of repentance and contrition may be quite familiar to many of us. In fact its very popularity is an indicator of our need to know how to express our remorse to God.

If you have read 2 Samuel 11 and 12, you are aware of the circumstances that brought David to this place of tragic confession, but the details are worth reviewing briefly before looking at the psalm itself. David finds himself comfortably at a loose end in Jerusalem while his armies are out fighting to maintain border security. He becomes infatuated with a soldier's wife and seduces her, making it necessary to

---

8. (Simon 1975)

arrange the death of her husband before he discovers she has become pregnant while he was on the front lines. Lust, adultery, conspiracy to murder; the whole episode reads like a soap opera! Nathan, a friend to David and a prophet of God, confronts the king and opens his eyes to his sins. The superscription to Psalm 51 tells us that those are the events we should keep in the back of our minds as we read this prayer.

Perhaps these are not the particular sins that weigh heavy on you, but the raw sentiments and emotions conveyed in this psalm are not limited to the sins of David. The petty thief, the tax dodger, the slanderer and the bully will need to stand before God regardless of whether they ever stand before a magistrate. Our conscience can be troubled by harsh words spoken, gossip shared, obscene thoughts entertained or grudges held too tight for too long. As we read in 1 John 1:8, the Apostle John is careful to point out:

> *If we say we have no sin, we deceive ourselves, and the truth is not in us.*

So, acknowledging that sin in its various manifestations is common to all mankind, how can we learn from David's prayer of repentance?

For a start, there's no time to lose and there are no words to waste. No polite preamble or beating around the bush. In two short verses, the prayer moves quickly to establish the key principles:

> *Have mercy on me, O God,*
> *according to your steadfast love;*
> *according to your abundant mercy*
> *blot out my transgressions.*
> *Wash me thoroughly from my iniquity,*
> *and cleanse me from my sin!*

First we are shown two vital components of God's character. His steadfast love and His abundant mercy (*you said . . . you could be trusted*). The contrast with Psalm 11 couldn't be greater. When we petition God to deal with the wicked and it's somebody else – we want His justice, and lots of it. We want Him to give *them* what's due. But just wait until we come to God with our own guilt: justice for the evildoer? – that's the last thing we are asking for! We don't want what's right, we want what's merciful. *Please Lord, as we start out dealing with my sin, don't lose sight of the fact that You have a reputation to uphold; a reputation for mercy and loyalty.*

The second notion that is laid on the table very quickly is the idea of urgency. David fires off a volley of four staccato orders to God. "Have mercy! Blot out! Wash me! Cleanse me!" These kinds of imperative commands are quite common in the Laments, and they sometimes sound a bit impudent to our ears. In fact the image here isn't a tentative knock at God's office door but more like throwing the door open, stepping up to His desk and demanding His attention. Such boldness might seem breathtaking but it gives evidence of a crucial factor here. There is an existing relationship already in place between the petitioner and the one who can give him relief. David knows God and God knows David. He is a "man after God's own heart" (1 Samuel 13:14 and Acts 13:22). When we know someone well, we can anticipate their reactions, we can know when to press and when to tread softly. David knows well enough that although his approach might seem brash and even risky, he trusts God to respond favourably; to understand that this is urgent business.

This liberty to approach God in times of trouble or joy is one of the most remarkable privileges granted to us in Christ. We are free at any time and on any occasion to approach Him as a child might run to their father about a grazed knee, a broken toy or with just a daisy from the garden. Paul describes such liberty with the words "confident access" in Ephesians 2:18 and 3:12. It signifies permission to approach at any time. No nervous hours in the waiting room, no need to take a number and hope to be called. We win this permission by being "in Christ." This is the phrase Paul uses to describe those of us who trust Jesus Christ to be the one who brings us into God's grace. Christ has, so to speak, made our introductions for us, but crucially He has also settled the matter of sin that had previously separated us from God.

"In Christ" we have certain guarantees, promises of what to expect from our relationship with God through Christ. And it is God's reputation for trustworthiness in the relationship that gives us our confidence when we approach Him. This trustworthiness on God's part is again picked up in 1 John 1:9:

> *If we confess our sins, he is faithful and just to forgive us our sins*
> *and to cleanse us from all unrighteousness.*

And this is the key to releasing our guilt as we come to Him in lament. So why didn't David just stop after these first two verses? Isn't that enough? "I'm a sinner, Lord, and you have an obligation to forgive me, because you promised." It sounds a bit shallow and superficial when we say it that way, right? And so it is. There is still soul-work to be done before we own our confession, and until we *own* our confession we cannot honestly own the forgiveness it brings.

David adds three verses that give proof to his ownership, and a further six verses where he thoughtfully considers a range of consequences. In broad terms, he is looking back at what has happened so far and forward to what he hopes will happen and what he fears could happen. He is in the process of working through his sin, coming to terms with himself and with the ramifications of his actions. It's a difficult, but important part of the process, this "coming to terms."

First we come to terms with ourselves. An honest appraisal isn't always pleasant, not when we consider ourselves as God sees us, rather than through our own rose-tinted glasses. David considers himself to be fully aware of his sinful nature. Presently, in his guilty state, it is always on his mind (v3). There is plain truth in this idea that once we become aware of our error, we find it hard to shake free of it until we have dealt with it. It colours every conversation, it intrudes on every relationship, it fills our daytime thoughts and imposes into our restless nights. It's actually the sign of a healthy soul. It is proof to the work of God's Spirit as He bears down on our self-understanding. You can't have a guilty conscience unless you really do have a conscience.

Verse four places two stark truths on the table: God is completely right, and all sin, any sin is wrong. What's more, any sin is ultimately an offence against Him. When we violate His will and His ways, it is to Him that we are accountable. But this introduces a practical problem as we deal with our sin. If we remember the circumstances of David's confession we can identify at least two victims – Bathsheba has been stalked and seduced; her husband Uriah has been killed. Does finding forgiveness from God relieve us of any consequences for our actions or free us from obligations to the victims of our actions? It is wrong to assume so. In fact finding forgiveness should be a strong motive for making good. In the previous chapter I referred to the principle that the repentant thief should work to become useful rather than harmful (Ephesians 4:28). Consider also Zacchaeus in Luke 19. His sin had been greed and forgiveness through salvation had prompted him to extravagant charity. The parable of the unforgiving servant teaches us that those who have been forgiven must themselves be willing to forgive. There are expectations placed on those who find forgiveness.

In addition to certain expectations, there are also consequences. We do not necessarily escape the earth-bound consequences of our sins. For David there was the death of the illegitimate child born to Bathsheba, and the steady unravelling of his family. In the chapters leading up to 2 Samuel 11, David's strength and influence is building to a crescendo. The nation is stable and prosperous. Following Nathan's pronouncement in 2 Samuel 12, having given up the moral high ground, David's authority is diminished, and the royal family descends into chaos. David's eldest son Amnon rapes his half-sister, and her full brother Absalom avenges her by murder. In time Absalom conspires to take the throne from his father, and is killed.

Certain decisions, certain rebellions, certain sins bring consequences that we cannot avoid. Legal judgments make a good example. A felon may be completely repentant for his crimes and may have found full forgiveness before God but he still has to serve his sentence. In the same way, sometimes infections or physical ailments can result from a foolish or rebellious approach to sexual activity. Complete forgiveness for promiscuity is offered in Christ but some consequences will nevertheless abide until the resurrection. The guilt is gone, but the damage is done and the regrets live on. Regrets are what we build wisdom upon – wisdom not to make the same mistake again; wisdom to warn others not to follow our example (v6).

In verses 7-12, we see David mulling through the consequences of his sin. What he wants to happen and what *could* happen are all present in his mind as he weighs the situation. He wants to be made clean, he wants to feel once again the joy of being right with God. He knows that his cleansing implies the shedding of blood: the "cleansing with hyssop" carries with it the idea of sacrificial sprinkling. The expression is used in Exodus 12:22 referring to the blood on the door posts and lintel at the Passover as well as with several cleansing rituals in the Law of Moses, a theme picked up again in Hebrews 9:19. What he wants is to be rid of his guilt so that he might enjoy fellowship with God again. It's what we all want when we come to our senses.

At the same time, David knows that God is sovereign, and He has some options:

> Cast me not away from your presence,
> and take not your Holy Spirit from me.

What if God would not want him back? David already understands the anxiety and pain of being alienated from God. He dreads the thought that he might never step back into the warmth of God's grace. Added to this, he fears that he might have forfeited the throne. That's the significance behind the removal of God's Holy Spirit. David was aware that God had removed His Spirit from his predecessor Saul (1 Samuel 16:13-14). Saul's sins had brought about his downfall. It would be a thousand years before the Church would be inaugurated at Pentecost. That moment marked the investment of God's Spirit into every believer. Before that, the Holy Spirit was given to specific people to perform specific tasks for God. In this way prophets, priests and kings were enabled by God to meet the demands of their office. The Spirit could be taken away if that office was abused. The right to function as God's agent could be rescinded.

Since Pentecost and the dawn of the Church Age, a true believer is not threatened with the removal of God's Spirit. Christ promised that once we are His we would never be left alone or forsaken. I do still take it, however, that the special empowerment needed to lead God's people can be revoked. That is not to forfeit one's salvation; it is to lose one's special gifting; to lose the great privilege of being used by God to influence the course of His work in the world. God is still sovereign, and He still has options. Those who might disgrace the privileges of leadership must understand that God will not be mocked.

In our psalm, the thought now moves from ideas of what *could* happen, to promises of what *will* happen if God relieves David of the burden of his guilt (verses 13-17).

Extravagant, enthusiastic but nonetheless honest praise sums up the emotion in this section. If God forgives David, he will make wisdom and instruction come out of it (sinners will be warned and taught God's ways). If God forgives David, he will make sure the whole world hears about it. But David has learned that lip-service is not enough. A changed heart is the result God wants to see. A heart that knows it is vulnerable and easily led astray; a heart that understands how it had become hardened against the truth; a heart that knows the agony of being estranged from God and wants only to follow Him out of this season of rebellion. With such a changed heart comes peace with God.

To my ear, the prayer closes in a very quiet, relaxed and undemanding tone. What a contrast to the frantic bluster at its opening! In His time God will bring the blessings of contrition and obedience. Order will be restored, the panic will die down. We will get back to going about things His way. For David, that means the usual course of sacrifices at the Tabernacle (the Temple has not yet been built). For us it might mean restored relationships with family, friends, or the local church. Restoration to fellowship with God makes the work of restoring fellowship with others possible. We never feel relaxed and "clean" in community unless we feel at ease with God.

How, Then, Should We Pray?

- *Waste no time!* When David realised his sin, he was compelled to deal with it. For perhaps a year he had not even realised his fault; it took the confrontation of a caring friend to open his eyes. Listen both to your conscience and to your friends. Don't assume that just because you're getting what you want, that it must be under God's blessing.

- *Own your confession to God.* This is not the time to be giving excuses or making rationalisations. "Here's what I have done, Lord – and I know it's wrong, I know you don't like it." If ever there was a time for emotional honesty, it's now. Don't try to bury your sins under a wagon-load of evasive words. God already knows what you have done but He wants to know that you see it clearly too. "I have not always respected the holy vows of matrimony I made before you in the presence of witnesses ..." is hedging. "I coveted and I lusted and I slept with another woman's husband, and now I am ashamed..." that's honest.

- **Take stock of the potential ramifications.** How will your sin affect those around you? Is there restitution to be made? The on-going consequences need to be owned honestly as well. If you have systematically betrayed your wife, she might leave you. You can ask God for help to know what to say to her. You might go to jail for embezzlement. That is a real consequence that you will need courage and grace to face. Ask God to help you to represent Him well while you serve out your time. You might find it necessary to step down from certain positions at the church, knowing in your soul that you should step away from leadership. Never will there be a sinful course of action that has no ramifications. Ask God to bring them to mind as He "creates a clean heart."

- **Claim the cleansing that is promised.** In Christ there is no unforgivable sin. God has promised to cleanse us of all unrighteousness if we confess our sins to Him.

- **Resolve to act in light of your forgiveness.** If your story can teach wisdom to anyone, be prepared to share it; many wrong steps can be avoided if we listen to those who have already tripped up. If there are relationships that need to be mended, do so humbly. If there are debts that need to be paid, make every effort. Your life is now a testimony to God's grace. Be sure to give Him all the credit for your restoration.

Conclusion

The rhythm of emotional honesty has been beating in the background all through this little book. That's because such honesty is at the very heart of the Psalms and particularly so in the Psalms of Lament. We shouldn't lose sight of the fact that God is thoroughly acquainted with our grievances and struggles. When we come to Him we are approaching one who already knows that we are struck down with soul-pain. Releasing our fears, our doubts, our shame to Him frees us from spiritual paralysis. It allows us to get on with what he has placed us here to do. To enjoy His loving kindness, and to represent Him well to a world that doesn't understand Him. My prayer is that – whether you come full of anxiety over a society that has lost its way or disappointed that life hasn't been easy for you or frantic in the wake of some sinful error – you will approach the throne of grace with boldness and confidence, secure in the knowledge that such privileged access has been granted to all of us who are called sons and daughters of God in His only Son, Jesus Christ.

Works Cited

Eareckson, Joni. *Joni*. Grand Rapids: Zondervan, 1976.

Eareckson, Joni, and Steve Estes. *A Step Further*. Grand Rapids: Zondervan, 1978.

Elliot, Elisabeth. *Keep A Quiet Heart*. Ventura CA: Vine Books, 1995.

—. *Loneliness*. Nashville: Oliver-Nelson Books, 1988.

Lewis, C. S. *A Grief Observed*. London: Faber and Faber, 1961.

Simon, Paul. "Some Folks' Lives Roll Easy." *Still Crazy After All These Years*. 1975.

Westermann, Claus. *The Psalms: Structure, Content & Message*. Translated by Ralph D. Gehrke. Minneapolis: Augsburg Publishing House, 1980.

We Are Here For You

If you desire to find out more about knowing God and His plan for you in the Bible, contact us. Insight for Living Ministries provides staff pastors who are available for free written correspondence or phone consultation. These seminary-trained and seasoned counsellors have years of experience and are well-qualified guides for your spiritual journey.

Please feel welcome to contact your regional office by using the information below:

United Kingdom and Europe

Insight for Living United Kingdom
Pastoral Care
PO Box 553
Dorking
RH4 9EU
UNITED KINGDOM
0800 787 9364
+44 (0)1306 640156
pastoralcare@insightforliving.org.uk

United States

Insight for Living
Biblical Counseling Department
Post Office Box 269000
Plano, Texas 75026-9000
USA
972-473-5097, Monday through Friday,
8:00 a.m. – 5:00 p.m. central time
www.insight.org /contactapastor

Canada

Insight for Living Canada
Biblical Counseling Department
PO Box 8 Stn A
Abbotsford BC V2T 6Z4
CANADA
1-800-663-7639
info@insightforliving.ca

Australia, New Zealand, and South Pacific

Insight for Living Australia
Pastoral Care
Post Office Box 443
Boronia, VIC 3155
AUSTRALIA
1300 467 444

Notes

Notes